Copyright © 2012 by Mary Lazier
First Edition – November 2012

ISBN
978-1-4602-0177-0 (Paperback)
978-1-4602-0178-7 (eBook)

All rights reserved.

No part of this publication may be reproduced in any form, or by any means, electronic or mechanical, including photocopying, recording, or any information browsing, storage, or retrieval system, without permission in writing from the publisher.

Published by:

FriesenPress
Suite 300 – 852 Fort Street
Victoria, BC, Canada V8W 1H8

www.friesenpress.com

Distributed to the trade by The Ingram Book Company

Stars Of Georgian Bay

BY MARY LAZIER

Dedication

*This book is gratefully dedicated to my husband Mark Tichenor,
the computer wizard who makes all things possible.*

Contents

Foreword by Judy Ross................................... vii
Ekarenniondi 1
Local Clay 2
Rachel's Collection..3
1616 Ste. Marie Among The Hurons 4
Jean de Brébeuf...5
The Black History Quilt Codes 6
The Sheffield Black History Museum 7
The Nancy 8
 Zebra Rocks..10
Zebra Rocks 11
By-Laws..12
The Town of Collingwood 13
W. Watts and Sons Boatbuilders 14
The Three Penny Beaver Stamp.........................16
Mr. Campbell 17
The Great Northern Exhibition 18
The Trott family 19
The Mary Ward 21
The Moberly Family 22
John McCormick 23
Murder 24
Elephants on Hurontario Street 25
Lighthouses..26
Lighthouses in Georgian Bay..........................27

Rescue!	28
Rough cast houses	29
Cutting Ice	31
The Ojibway Hotel	32
Billy Bishop	34
Orville Wright	35
First Ski Lift at Blue Mountain	37
Blue Mountain Pottery	38
Tom Thomson	40
Milkweed	41
The Little Red Hen Restaurant	42
The Search for the Girl with the Blue Eyes	43
Sidelaunchings	44
Premier Bill Davis	46
Sister ships	47
Tuzo Wilson	48
Wye Marsh and Pig Pen	49
Charles Garrad	51
The Eastern Massasauga Rattlesnake	52
The Elvis Festival	54
The Flower Lady	**55**
TugFest	56
Acknowledgements	57
Bibliography	59

Foreword by Judy Ross

In this endearing book, we are taken on a merry romp around Georgian Bay. Along the way we discover amazing characters and quirky stories. We learn about elephants parading down the main street of Collingwood, and we meet a farmer who played the bagpipes on the roof of his shanty in order to scare off intruders. As well, there's the fruitful Pig Pen, a famous trumpeter swan from the Wye Marsh near Midland.

Author and illustrator Mary Lazier has uncovered many charming stories. So many, in fact, that a lot of the oddball details were new to me, even though I've lived in Collingwood for over a decade and have written two books on the Georgian Bay area.

I have known Mary for many years and have admired her work as a potter. Now it seems, she has added talents - the journalist's ear for a good story and the illustrator's eye for the telling detail. Her delightful illustrations, part of a new direction in her life as an artist, richly enhance her written vignettes.

This book will be treasured by anyone interested in Georgian Bay's history and characters. And it is sure to provide cocktail conversation for years to come.

Judy Ross, Collingwood, Ontario

Ekarenniondi

Ekarenniondi means "the rock that stands out" and is also known as "The Watcher". This is a standing rock located at the Scenic Caves five miles west of Collingwood. In the mythology of the Ouendat, it was the marker for the path to the village of the souls or "the afterlife". The Ouendat believed that on the way to the afterlife they had to pass Oscatarah, the head-piercer who removed their brains. Ekarenniondi was considered to be a living rock - it was magical - and meant something different to different people. Some people say that Ekarenniondi was consecrated by Jean de Brébeuf.

Local Clay

The pot on the left was made by the the Ouendat People, and is the oldest intact pot from their culture. It resides in the ROM in Toronto. The pot on the right is a Blue Mountain Pottery creation, made a thousand years later. The source of the clay for both pots was the Blue Mountains.

980 AD   1980 AD

Rachel's Collection

This is a Laurentide ancient peoples' spear tip. Made of chert, archaeologist Charles Garrad estimated it to be 5000 years old.

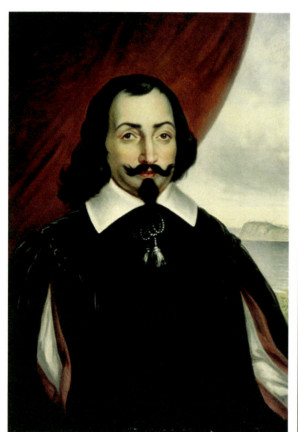 

1616 Ste. Marie Among The Hurons

This site at Midland re-creates the French Jesuit Settlement from 1639-1649. Champlain brought Étienne Brûlé to Canada in 1610 to become the first "Coureur des Bois" (he was probably the first European to visit Georgian Bay). He learned the language and customs of the Aboriginal people, and actually came to look like them. Champlain was intent on trading beaver pelts, and exploring western Canada with the hope of finding "The Great Western Sea" and Asia. He was also the Governor of New France and the founder of Quebec City.

To get to Huronia, the canoes had to travel up the Ottawa River to the Magnetawan, through Lake Nipissing and down The French River to Georgian Bay. There were fifty portages in the eight hundred mile route. Champlain visited Huronia in 1616.

Jean de Brébeuf

In 1626, Jean de Brébeuf made the long journey to Toanché near Midland in Penetanguishene Bay, where he learned the customs and language of the Ouendat people. He called the Ouendat "The Huron" and he wrote the first Huron dictionary and the Huron Carol, "Twas in the Moon of Wintertime". He tried to Christianize the Ouendat, and in 1639, he built the village "Ste. Marie Among the Hurons" across the Bay at a site on the Wye River.

Although he spoke several native languages, none had words for Heaven, Hell, the devil or Jesus Christ, so Christian tenets were hard to teach. By 1636, Brébeuf had converted eighty-six Ouendat: - by 1647 there were thousands more. The settlement held French and Christianized Ouendat, plus a few who did not embrace the faith but were helpful to the Black Robe Missionaries. Unfortunately the Europeans brought terrible diseases with them, including smallpox. The Black Robes baptized the dying, and the Aboriginal people began to believe that the French were killing them and stealing their souls.

The Ouendat fought the Six Nations over the fur trade, and in a raid on March 16, 1649, Brébeuf and Gabrielle Lallement were captured and killed. After another raid on Ste. Marie, the remaining French and Ouendat escaped to Christian Island where most of them died the first winter of starvation.

The Black History Quilt Codes

These bits of sewn cloth showed the escaping slaves how to get to Canada safely.

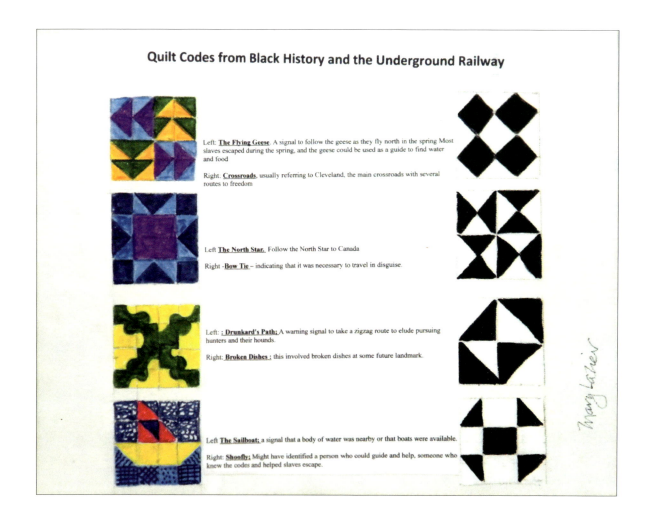

The Sheffield Black History Museum

The museum is located in Clarksburg at 241 Clark Street. It was started by historian Howard Sheffield and his niece Carolynn Wilson. The Sheffields were United Empire Loyalists who were given free land in Canada after helping the British in the American War of Independence in 1776.

Collingwood was also the end of the Underground Railway which assisted slaves on their trip to freedom in Canada. It was the Quaker people who opposed slavery and started the Underground Railway. They kept safe-houses and provided shelter, food, money and conveyances for assistance. Howard said that many of the early black settlers intermarried with First Nations people. He commented, "It's not often said, but next to the First Nations, we were the first to arrive here, and the proof is in our features", proudly standing sideways so the noble-looking hook of his nose was visible.

The Nancy

The Nancy was a schooner, built by the British in 1789 of oak and red cedar, and she was important in the fur trade and the War of 1812. She took supplies such as rum, food, clothing, weapons and ammunition to Collingwood and Sault Ste. Marie. She returned with furs to Mackinak Island near the junction of Lake Huron and Lake Michigan where the British Fort Michilimackinac was located. During the War of 1812, she was fitted with guns and participated in Brock's capture of Detroit. She was scuttled by three American ships at the end of the War of 1812 and sank at Wasaga Beach, in the Nottawasaga River on August 14 1814, while under the command of Lieutenant Worsely. On August 31, the captain and ninety-two men in four rowboats rowed 360 miles to Fort Michilimackinac to avenge the sinking of the Nancy. They captured the Tigress and the Scorpion, the two ships that had brought the Nancy down. There is now a museum in honour of the Nancy in Wasaga Beach.

Zebra Rocks

These rocks are called "banded gneiss formation", and are visible at various places around the bay. The stripes were formed when black basalt rock became soft as toothpaste from heat during the Silerian Period, four-hundred million years ago, and the black basalt mixed with white quartzite but they didn't blend together.

Metamorphic rocks, however, blended two colours of molten rock to produce the pink rocks of Georgian Bay - red feldspar combined with quartzite.

By-Laws

Early in the history of Collingwood, a by-law to prevent animals from roaming the streets was hotly debated in the local press. Proponents of the by-law said that animals on the streets left mountains of manure which smelled terrible and attracted flies and other vermin. Against the by-law were the animal owners who were too busy and too poor to erect fences on their property. One letter, defending the animals said, "Why, In the name of right, should cows be kept off town streets? Are they not amongst our soberest citizens? Do they howl profane and vulgar epithets outside the hotels after dark?"

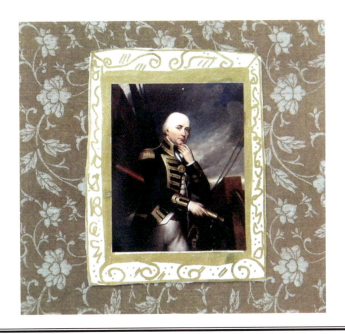

The Town of Collingwood

The town of Collingwood was originally called "Hen and Chickens Harbour", but when the railway line was planned to come north from Toronto, it was decided that a more dignified name was necessary for the future "Chicago of the North". Admiral Collingwood was famous at the time for his naval career from 1760 to 1810. He was born in Newcastle Upon Tyne, England, in 1748, and first went to sea when he was eleven years old. Eventually he became captain of The Royal Sovereign, which, along with Horatio Nelson, fought the battle of Trafalgar against Napoleon Bonaparte and the French and Spanish navies in 1805. Collingwood became commander-in-chief when Nelson died. He was awarded three gold medals for service during the Napoleonic Wars. Some say it was John Moberly of the Royal Navy who named the town. This portrait by Henry Howard can be seen at Greenwich Hospital in England.

W. Watts and Sons Boatbuilders

The Watts brothers, Matthew and William, arrived in Canada from Sligo County Ireland in about 1842. They were trained boat builders, and the area of Collingwood, (or "Hen and Chickens Harbour" as it was then called), attracted them because of the water, the woods, and the proposed railway which was finished in 1855. The brothers began a tradition of wooden-boat building that lasted over one hundred years, and pre-dated the steel ship-building business by thirty years.

In 1862, Matthew Watts left Collingwood and settled in Goderich. William took over the business and built fishing boats, barges, schooners, lifeboats and scows, all considered to be extremely seaworthy. They used oak for the ribs and cedar for the planking; they had two to three hundred pound centre boards. Apparently they were such skilled craftsmen that many boats were built by eye and intuition, without plans or drawings. The Watts built skiffs were double-ended, lap-streak with a shallow draft, mostly used for fishing.

The Three Penny Beaver Stamp

Canadian beaver pelts were popular in the early 1600s because of the European gentlemen's fashion of wearing top hats made of beaver pelts. Samuel Champlain's mission had as much to do with finding a source of beaver fur as it did with finding cod fish and Asia. Canadian beaver pelts were prized because they were heavier and silkier due to the cold winters.

Until 1850s, the stamps used in Canada were British. The "Three Penny Beaver" issued in 1851 was Canada's first stamp. It was designed by Sir Sandford Fleming, to celebrate the beaver's industrious nature and important financial contribution to the founders of Canada. Sir Sandford didn't live on Georgian Bay, but his parents and brothers did, having emigrated in 1845. Craigleith was named after the Scottish quarry near Edinburgh, where the family originated - it means rocky bay in Gaelic.

Mr. Campbell

Alarmed by some passing Ouendat who were digging his potatoes, Mr. Campbell decided to scare them off by playing his bagpipes on the roof of his shanty. The Ouendat weren't scared at all, but rather, loved the music and started to dance.

The Great Northern Exhibition

Established in 1885, this picture shows the original building, with the school children marching in a parade. They got Friday afternoon off school and got into the fair free that day.

The Trott family

The Trott Family were pioneers in Collingwood, and it is said that the first members of the family stuffed mattresses with swamp grass. They were cabinet makers, and (naturally in those days) they made coffins and had a funeral home. When the Collingwood Shipyards set up business, the Trott family outfitted the ships from top to bottom, often having to build custom shapes and sizes to fit odd interior angles.

The Trott Building was built in 1867 in the "Venetian Style" and originally housed the whole business, furniture showrooms, a hearse house and coffin storage.

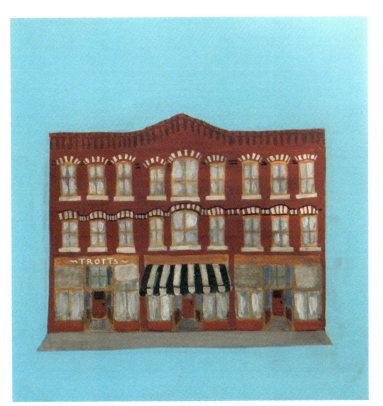

Samuel Trott Sr. arrived in Canada from New York in 1843. He was an English cabinet maker. Five generations of Samuel's descendants who ran the business are listed below.

Samuel Trott Jr. also a cabinet maker arrived in Collingwood 1862.

Henry, cabinet maker

Harry Trott born 1872

Clare Trott born 1898

Jim Trott born 1924, he closed the business when the Shipyards closed in 1986.

The Mary Ward

On the night of November 24, 1872, the steamer Mary Ward ran aground on Milligan's Reef near Craigleith. The first lifeboat reached shore but a fierce gale delayed rescue. The second lifeboat landed safely but the third went down, and all eight aboard drowned.

Frank Moberly walked from Craigleith to Collingwood, hoping to borrow a tug from his brother George. However, the tug was in dry dock for the winter, so Frank took the train to Thornbury and led a group of eight local fishermen to heroically rescue those remaining on board. A medal was struck to honour the bravery and persistence of Frank Moberly.

The Moberly Family

Frank Moberly came from an interesting family. His father John was born in St Petersburg Russia, in 1789, and was a captain of the Royal Navy, later stationed at Penetanguishene from 1833 on. Frank's mother was Marie Foch, a Russian aristocrat, who was adopted and raised by Czar Nicholas 1st when her father, a Russian General, was killed at the battle of Borodino. The Moberly family of ten lived in a rough hewn log house, but according to Charles Garrad, they had a full set of Dickens to read on the long winter nights. Frank's brother George was mayor of Collingwood, and his brother Clarence was a civil engineer. John Moberly is said by some to have named Collingwood.

John McCormick

John McCormick was an upstanding gentleman of the Catholic faith who built the Tremont Hotel at 80 Simcoe Street in 1889. In later life he lived with his sister, and he had a pet parrot. The parrot learned some terribly foul language from a local farmer, which was very embarrassing to Mr. McCormick. He had to catch the bird and put it in its cage under a blanket when guests arrived.

Murder

When the jail in Owen Sound was first built in 1890, Cook Teets was the first man hanged, accused of murdering his wife with strychnine poison. His mother-in-law confessed to the crime twenty years later.

Elephants on Hurontario Street

The elephants on Hurontario Street were part of the Hodgson Circus, around 1890. Frederick A. Hodgson was a local architect, whose son Frederick A. was a circus agent and owner. Fredrick A. was married to Carrie Hodgson who taught dance. In the off-season, the family had exotic visitors, including Mr. Ringling and the President of Mexico. They entertained the local populace with many impromptu performances. Their daughter Jessica taught dance, rode bareback in the circus and eventually danced with the Zeigfield Follies.

Lighthouses

The first light house was built in 270 B.C. in Alexandria Egypt. It was one of the seven wonders of the ancient world – at four-hundred feet high, it could be seen for thirty-three miles. The Romans built about thirty lighthouses around the Mediterranean.

Early light sources were wood fires and oil lamps which used whale oil -some oil lamps had as many as 12 wicks, so there had to be people to maintain them -often in very remote locations. The Fresnel lens pictured here was invented in 1822, and it used concentric circles of thin lenses in a ring. Prisms focused the light and reflectors increased the brightness. The Fresnel lens allowed light which would otherwise be diffused to be focused on a horizontal plane in all directions. The lighthouses had individual flash patterns so the navigators could tell which light they were seeing in bad weather.

Lighthouses in Georgian Bay

In 1881, the first keeper of the light on Georgian Bay was Charles Earl, who was paid one hundred dollars per year to manage a lantern on Big Tub Island.

The lighthouse-building project started in 1858. The lamps used to light the lighthouses used sperm whale blubber oil, which later evolved to turnip oil and kerosene before electric lights arrived in the 1970s. There were over fifty lighthouses on Manitoulin and Georgian Bay, but the number of ships declined from fifteen a day to four, and with the advent of radar, eventually the lighthouse-keepers and their families left and many of the original lighthouses were destroyed, although some have remained to remind us of their long history.

Rescue!

Around 1940, in Blantyre, Milford Sewell saved his valuable imported English bathtub off the porch when his house caught on fire.

Rough cast houses

Rough-cast houses were built during the Great Depression. After the building was complete, the outside was covered with a thick lime cement, and while it was still wet, pebbles were thrown from a blanket against the wall where they stuck. It is hard to find these houses because they were painted, and look like regular stucco houses.

Cutting Ice

Cutting Ice from the bay was a tough winter occupation before refrigeration, and special tools were required for the job. Sleighs, horses, ramps, pulleys and brute strength were needed to get enough ice into the ice huts or under buildings to last the summer. The ice was preserved in sawdust, and one waitress at the Ojibway Hotel thought gin and tonic always had to have a bit of sawdust added to make it authentic.

The Ojibway Hotel

The Ojibway Hotel was built "in the rustic style" by Hamilton Davis, and it opened in June of 1906. It was a great success immediately, with guests arriving from Chicago, Cleveland and Toronto for month long stays. They came on steamers before the railway reached Pointe au Baril. The Ojibway is now called The Ojibway Club.

Billy Bishop

Billy Bishop (1894-1956) was a famous World War One flying ace who grew up in Owen Sound. He was an unremarkable student, but as a pilot his bravery was unsurpassed. He flew a Sopwith Camel and chased down Germans, including Baron von Richtofen (The Red Baron). He hated the Germans passionately because they killed so many of his friends.

He was awarded many medals, six of them shown here. From the upper left, the Victoria Cross for most exceptional bravery in presence of the enemy, the Military Cross for shooting down 12 aircraft in one day, the Distinguished Service Order, the Distinguished Flying Cross, the Croix de Guerre and the Legion d' Honneur. He survived the war even though the average life span of a young pilot was only 11 days. He died in Florida.

Orville Wright

Orville Wright was born in Dayton Ohio on August 19 1871. He was the first man to make and fly a "powered flight machine" at Kitty Hawk North Carolina, on Dec 17, 1903. He stayed aloft for twelve seconds. He and his brother Wilbur were the super stars of the time, travelling all over the world to demonstrate their aircraft which improved rapidly to a two-passenger long distance airplane.

Orville Wright owned Lambert Island at Cognashene which he bought from William Cawthra, who never built on the island because his wife could not be persuaded to get out of the boat to see it. A keen fisherman and dinghy sailor, Wright drove this 1929 Gidley Gull motor launch called The KITTYHAWK, and he often entertained the famous painter A.Y. Jackson, among other luminaries of the time

First Ski Lift at Blue Mountain

According to Herb Hall in Christine Cowley's "Butchers Bakers and Building the Lakers," Voices of Collingwood, the first ski lift at Blue Mountain was a sleigh pulled backwards up the mountain by six Clydesdale horses. Then came The Red Devil ski lift, pulled by a Buick engine.

Blue Mountain Pottery

In an interview with Collingwood's Newspaper The Enterprise, July 23 2004, Dennis Tupy told his version of the origin of Blue Mountain Pottery. He had escaped from the Czechoslovakian army during WWll and found a job in Canada on a farm near Beaver Valley which paid forty-five dollars a month. Jozo Weider, also a Czech refugee, found Dennis and told the farmer he was taking him away. Dennis was willing to go because Jozo spoke Czech and offered him more money. Jozo gave Dennis room and board plus eighty cents an hour.

While they were preparing ski runs on the mountain, they found deposits of clay. When Jozo asked Dennis what could be done with clay, Dennis said, "Make pottery!" Dennis had learned pottery skills in Europe and he took over development of Blue Mountain Pottery - while Jozo acted as the businessman and built electric kilns to fire the work. Tupy didn't copy anyone's work, he considered himself "Gifted by the Lord".

The first pottery studio was in the basement of the ski barn in 1949.

Tom Thomson

Tom Thomson was a famous landscape painter who was aligned with The Group of Seven. He was raised in Leith, near Owen Sound. He was born in 1878, and died mysteriously in 1917 in Canoe Lake, Algonquin Park, where he had painted for years. His body was found with a bad injury to his temple, and he had a fishing line deliberately wrapped around his ankle. His body wasn't found for a week after his gray-blue canoe was found upturned on the lake, causing some people to think that he had been murdered and weighted down by the line around his ankle that was tied to a rock.

Roy MacGregor in Northern Light suggests that Tom Thomson had had a fist-fight the night before he died, and fell against the fireplace knocking himself out. He speculates that the proprietor of the lodge disposed of the body to avoid a charge of murder.

Milkweed

During the WWII, children helped by picking milkweed, which was used to stuff life preservers.

41

The Little Red Hen Restaurant

The Little Red Hen Restaurant opened in 1955, and the daughter of the owner was the manager. She had her office in the outhouse, which had one of the few flush toilets in the area at the time.

The Search for the Girl with the Blue Eyes

Published in 1968, The Search for the Girl with the Blue Eyes tells the tale of Joanne MacIver who was hypnotized by her father. While hypnotized, she told of a previous life as a pioneer named Susan Ganier, in 1848 near Morley on the St. Vincent-Sydenham town line. Under hypnosis, she led the writer Jess Stearn and his Doubleday editor David Manuel to the site of the ruins of her house, barn and well. She gave names of friends and the post mistress Mrs. Speedy, which were later confirmed.

Sidelaunchings

Sidelaunchings at Collingwood Shipyards were unique in that a ship would be launched sideways into a launch basin one hundred and twenty-five feet wide. The ship, about seventy-five feet in width, would be built atop a launchways which was parallel to the basin. The launchways, erected on the ground, involved giant timbers which were perpendicular to the launch basin and spaced far apart enough to give two men swinging sledge hammers access under the ship. On launch day, thousands of spectators would crowd every available shoreline space; sometimes standing on equipment, or rooftops for a better view. Children often got the day off school to come and see the spectacle of a sidelaunch. Invited dignitaries got the closest view, usually from a specially-built viewing stand. On launch day, a rally gang of two-hundred men would pound wedges in between timbers of the launchways under the ship. The wedges were hammered into place underneath the side of the ship furthest away from the launch basin, and a morning's work would raise that side of the ship slightly. The idea was to break gravity's hold.

At precisely the correct moment, with all workers safely out of the way, the launchmaster would signal and the ship's slide sideways would begin. The ship's hull would taste the water of the Great Lakes for the first time and the hull's displacement would send a massive wave eastward flooding nearby property and what is now called Heritage Drive. Huge chains would snap taut to stop the ship from going too far across the launch basin. The sidelaunch itself would take from seven to ten seconds. It took about six to eight months to build a ship to the sidelaunch stage.

By George Czerny

45

Premier Bill Davis

In 1972, Premier Bill Davis came to the Craigleith Depot. He was allowed to drive the train, but unfortunately the engineer forgot to take the brake off. An arch which was to display lilacs interfered with underground communication cables and the train set off all the red lights and clangors for miles. The train couldn't move after that, so Mr. Davis was driven to Meaford in the rain for another appointment. By the time he got there, everyone had gone home.

Sister ships

Sister ships, The Assinaboia and Keewatin were ordered by the Russian government, were built on the Clyde River in Scotland. Russia couldn't pay for them so Canada bought them. When they arrived in Montreal they were too long to go through the locks, so they were cut in half and towed to Buffalo, where they were re-assembled and painted.

Tuzo Wilson

Dr. Wilson was a world renowned Geophysicist and he commissioned a Chinese Junk built in Hong Kong in 1962, which was delivered to Toronto Harbour on the deck of a Japanese freighter. When he ordered it, he said the name would be The Peking Duck, but the builder said that would be inappropriate, in Chinese it would be similar to calling an English boat The Roast Beef. Dr. Wilson conceded, and changed the name to The Mandarin Duck, which he sailed out of Go Home Bay.

Wye Marsh and Pig Pen

The Wye Marsh near Minden is a 2500 acre bird sanctuary dedicated to saving the trumpeter swan from extinction. The marsh and wetland also harbours frogs, black terns and least bitterns.

Pig Pen was a female trumpeter swan who hatched at The Wye in 1990, the first surviving cygnet from the original captive pair. She was released into the wild in 1991, and was the first to nest in two-hundred years, establishing the first natural migration of these swans in Ontario. Pig Pen produced over seventy descendants, but died in 2001 after she was hit by a boat.

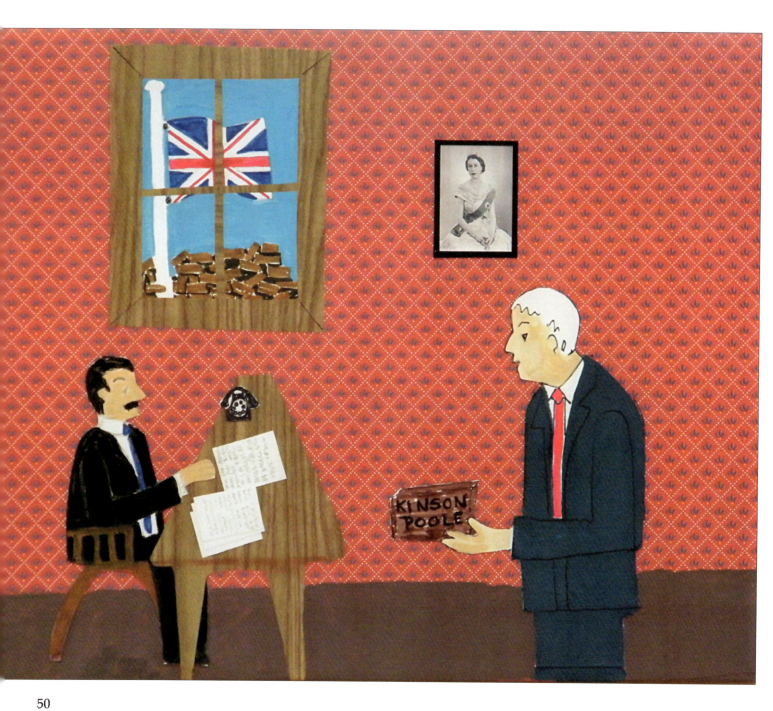

Charles Garrad

Charles Garrad is a well-known local archaeologist with a special interest in the native people of the Georgian Bay area. He found an old brick at the ruins of the Shale Oil Works site at Craigleith. Thinking that it might be of historical interest, he took it to England in his briefcase. The director of Kinson Poole (a company that had been in business since Roman Times) said, "Thanks, we have a ruddy great pile of them out back if you want more."

According to Charlie, the Kinson Poole bricks were specially made "flue bricks" which could withstand the great heat at the Shale Oil Works.

The Eastern Massasauga Rattlesnake

This is the only venomous snake in Ontario, and warns its victims with a rattle at the end of its tail. Its name means "it has a big mouth." Adults feed on mice, voles and frogs. Anyone bitten should go to the closest hospital as soon as possible for a shot of antivenom.

At one time there was a still at Stokes Bay and when the police raided it they were afraid for their lives when Meg Bradley, the daughter of the brewer, threatened them by flailing rattlesnakes at them.

The Elvis Festival

Hundreds of tribute artists have been celebrating Elvis annually since 1995. Every year it gets bigger and better, starting with a street party on the third Friday in July.

The Flower Lady

A cheerful Collingwood sight.

TugFest

This is an annual festival celebrating tug boats. It is held in a different location every year.

Acknowledgements

This book follows Stars of Dufferin, which was published in 2010. It was so much fun that I was working on this one before the first was even printed. So many great people came to my assistance - Christine Cowley's book, "Butchers Bakers and Building the Lakers": Voices of Collingwood, gave me the side launch, collecting milkweed, the rough cast house, Clydesdale horses pulling the skiers up the mountain. Christine also remembered two great stories - Mr. McCormick and his rude parrot, and the office in the outhouse at Little Red Hen Restaurant.

Charlie Garrad looked the book over, corrected a few statements, and made some suggestions. He suggested adding some details about Frank Moberly's mother, Marie Foch, who was a Russian aristocrat. Stephen Thomas sent the picture of the arrowhead from his daughter Rachel's collection, plus permission to use it and the text.

Instead of Indian or Huron, I have used Ouendat (their original name), which means "Dwellers of the Peninsula" or "Islanders". The word Huron was applied by the French and is now considered outdated. Thanks to Ruth Koleszar-Green for advice on political correctness.

The Zebra Rocks initially came from a David Suzuki Geology of Time CD, and that information was added to by Ed Bartram, a painter and printmaker who owns an island near Pointe Au Baril.

It was a rainy day when I went to see the jail in Owen Sound with Tish Russell. We walked the perimeter, taking photographs, and when we got back to the car we were surrounded by two fully loaded policemen who demanded to know our business. Luckily I knew the story about Cook Teets from Ray Argyle at a writing course I had taken in 2010, so they allowed us to leave without any trouble.

The text for the sidelaunch was delivered by e-mail from George Czerny.

Susan Wilson, the daughter of Dr. Tuzo Wilson, was a great help with the shape and rigging of the Chinese Junk. Thanks also to Rosemarie O'Brien for the Elvis information, and The Craigleith Depot Museum. Carolynn Wilson kindly approved the text of the Sheffield Museum.

Thanks to Barb Hall, Donna Lang, Maureen Dunn, Raymond Fahey and Gloria Culbert for lending me books.

Thanks to Tish Russell and Dean Dewey for many wonderful lunches!

You may ask,

"Did all these things really happen Mary?"

"Yes they did, more or less"

"Are you saying that some things have been invented?"

"Things are always invented in the telling of a story"

Bibliography

Blaise Clark, Time Lord, Vintage Canada
Cotton Larry D., Whiskey and Wickedness volume 4 by Larry D. Cotton
Cowley Christine, Butchers Bakers and Building the Lakers, Voices of Collingwood, Lifegems Personal Histories
Collingwood Township, The End of an Era 1977-1997
Cranson Herbert J., Huronia, Cradle of Ontario's History by Huronia Museum
Crompton and Rhein, The Ultimate Book of Lighthouses
Council of the Township of Collingwood, Collingwood Township
Czerny George, A Salute to Sidelaunchings by Blurb Inc
Derry, Margaret E., Georgian Bay Jewel
Floren and Gutsche Ghosts of the Bay by Lynx Images
Gutsche, Chisholm and Floren, Alone in the Night by Lynx Images
Johnstone Guy R., From Kitty Hawk to KITTYHAWK by Huronia Museum
Leitch Adelaide, Illustrated History of Simcoe County
Macfarlane David, At The Ojibway
Mathieson W.D., Billy Bishop VC, Fitzhenry and Whiteside Limited
Ross Judy and John de Visser, A View of the Bay Boston Mills Press
Stearn, Jess, The Search for the Girl with the Blue Eyes Doubleday
Suzuki David, a CD called Geologic Journey
Tupy, Dennis from The Enterprise July 23 2004.
Weider, George, Blue Mountain by Boston Mills Press
Wickens Lucilla. Thornbury Remembered
Wright, Larry and Patricia, Great Lakes Lighthouses